THE
MCFADDIN-WARD HOUSE

Library of Congress Cataloging-in-Publication Data

Foy, Jessica H.
  The McFaddin-Ward house / by Jessica H. Foy and Judith W. Linsley.
    p.   cm.   —(Popular history series ; no. 6)
  Includes bibliographical references.
  ISBN 0-87611-117-7 (paperback : acid free paper)
    1. McFaddin-Ward House Museum. 2. Architecture, Domestic—Texas—
  Beaumont. 3. Beaumont (Tex.)—Buildings, structures, etc. 4. McFaddin family.
  5. Beaumont (Tex.)—Social life and customs. 6. Beaumont (Tex.)—Biography.
  I. Linsley, Judith Walker.   II. Title.   III. Series.
  F394.B3F68   1992
  976.4'145—dc20

Number six in the Popular History Series
ISBN: 0-87611-117-7
Design by David Timmons

Published by the Texas State Historical Association in cooperation with the
Center for Studies in Texas History at the University of Texas at Austin.

Cover: McFaddin-Ward House, 1988. *Courtesy* Texas Highways.

CONTENTS

THE
MCFADDIN-WARD
HOUSE

BY JESSICA H. FOY
AND JUDITH W. LINSLEY

TEXAS STATE
HISTORICAL ASSOCIATION

INTRODUCTION

THE FIRST ANGLO SETTLERS to make their way to Texas were hardy individuals—men and women of boundless energy, strong convictions, and often unconventional ideas. Given a chance at a new life, they were determined to make it a good one and from the beginning took an active role in the community, leaving a trail of their activities on the pages of early records. Thus their stories, and those of their descendants, were inextricably intertwined with those of the towns they helped to create.

Two such early settlers were James McFaddin and his wife Elizabeth, who came in 1833 to live on the west bank of the Neches River, near what would later become the town of Beaumont. As the town grew, so did the McFaddin fortunes, and James and Elizabeth's son William, a veteran of the Battle of San Jacinto, built an empire of cattle and land. In his turn, William's son William Perry Herring McFaddin (WPH, or Perry to his friends) not only augmented the land and cattle business but diversified McFaddin interests to include rice farming and milling, meat packing, fur trapping, and commercial real estate.

In the last years of the nineteenth century, the town of Beaumont enjoyed a period of economic prosperity, ushered in by the growth of the railroads and the subsequent expansion of the lumber, cattle, and rice industries. With prosperity came a desire to possess the very best that life had to offer, and wealthy Beaumonters pointed their efforts, and their funds, to developing an active social and cultural life for themselves and their families. Desiring their homes to reflect their economic success, they built fine Victorian mansions in elegant neighborhoods. One of the most elegant of these neighborhoods was situated along Calder Avenue, which led west out of Beaumont in the direction of William McFaddin's homestead.

The discovery of oil in 1901 at Spindletop, near Beaumont, brought a new source of wealth to the town and doubled the population, creating a need for even more high-income housing. The Calder Avenue neighborhood, consisting of Calder and the avenues paralleling it on both sides—Broadway, Liberty, McFaddin, North, Hazel, and Harrison, to name a few—eventually overtook the boundaries of William McFaddin's land. By then the original McFaddin survey had been subdivided into the McFaddin and Averill additions, and new homes began to fill the empty lots.

One of the grandest of these homes, built in 1905–1906 and located at 1906 McFaddin Avenue, eventually became a new home for W. P. H. and Ida McFaddin. As the Calder Avenue neighborhood came into its prime during the first part of the twentieth century, the McFaddins' home enjoyed a heyday as well, its imposing appearance serving as the perfect backdrop to Ida McFaddin's frequent entertaining. Later, the McFaddins' daughter Mamie McFaddin Ward followed her mother's example, acting as gracious hostess for many elegant functions held at the home.

During Mrs. Ward's lifetime, the neighborhood surrounding the McFaddin-Ward House gradually changed. With the construction in the 1950s and 1960s of suburban shopping centers and the interstate highway that bypassed the central city, the population moved outward and the once-stylish Calder Avenue area began to settle into old age. Yet Mrs. Ward continued to keep her home as she had, devotedly maintaining its turn-of-the-century beauty.

As some of the homes along Calder were torn down to make way for small office buildings, the area took on a commercial appearance. Eventually, however, merchants came to appreciate the architectural and aesthetic value of the old homes and chose to utilize them rather than rebuild. Craftsmen, artists, and restaurateurs began to restore and renovate their places of business, and the aging neighborhood took on a new life as a historic district.

Mamie McFaddin Ward died in 1982, and, according to her wishes, her home became the McFaddin-Ward House Museum, opening to the public in 1986. A prominent structure in this historic neighborhood, the McFaddin-Ward House represents a chapter in the history of the McFaddin family, a history linked closely with that of Beaumont itself. It also serves as a reminder of the day when it was just one of many grand homes that lined the streets of Beaumont. The scale and design of the home itself reflect the prosperity of the family and the town, as well as prevailing aesthetic trends, at the turn of the century. Most important, however, is its role, not as a showplace, but as a family dwelling. Children grew up in the house; guests came and went; and the fundamental activities of day-to-day life—eating, sleeping, working, playing—occurred as in any other home. So the house provides a history, not just of a building, but of early twentieth-century life. To this end, it is being preserved and made accessible to the public, thanks to the foresight and provisions of its last resident owner, Mamie McFaddin Ward.

1.
THE McFADDIN FAMILY

IN 1821, THE YEAR THAT MEXICO won its independence from Spain, the Mexican government authorized colonization in Mexican Texas, and later that year Missourian Stephen F. Austin, in the role of empresario, brought in the first Anglo settlers. As a precaution, however, the government discouraged settlement in southeast Texas between the Sabine River (then the border between Mexico and the United States) and the Trinity River. Empresarios took their colonists past this area to land grants in the interior of the state. In this way, a sort of buffer zone was unofficially created between Mexico and the United States.

Following Austin's Old Three Hundred, as the original colonists were called, other Anglo-American settlers flocked to the rich new land to seek their fortunes. Many came to Texas along the Atascosito, or Opelousas, Trail, which followed the high ground from southwestern Louisiana into the interior. As the early colonists passed through the buffer zone, the vast forests and lush coastal prairies no doubt tempted them to stay. Most of them, however, preferring an empresario's leadership, pressed on until they reached the designated area. Only a few bolder ones chose to trust their own luck and settled in the unauthorized territory.[1]

One of these bold men was James McFaddin. A native of Tennessee, he had come first to Louisiana, where in 1815 he fought in the Battle of New Orleans and, sometime before 1819, married Elizabeth Mackey, whom one census listed as being from North Carolina.[2] In 1823 the couple migrated to Texas with their children to settle in the Atascosito settlement at Moss Bluff, now part of Liberty County.

Others soon followed. Governmental restrictions notwithstanding, the rich buffer area continued to attract settlers, and its population grew along with that of the authorized colonies. In 1827 the residents of the Atascosito settlement applied to the Mexican government for permission to become a colony. In 1828 the application was approved, and in 1829 empresarios were at last assigned lands that lay in the buffer zone, thus officially opening them for colonization. On April 26, 1831, James McFaddin obtained title to his league of land from the Mexican government. In 1833, however, he left Moss Bluff, retracing his steps eastward to settle in what eventually would become Jefferson County.[3]

James McFaddin chose his second homesite well, for it lay not only at the conjunction of forest and prairie, but also near the point where the Atascosito Trail crossed the Neches River. There, two tiny communities perched on the riverbank: Tevis Bluff, settled in 1824 by the area's first Anglo settler, Noah Tevis; and just downstream, the townsite of Santa Anna, named for the president of Mexico. James McFaddin located his survey on the river just north of Noah Tevis. There he built a log cabin and began to farm and raise cattle.

Meanwhile, settlers continued to arrive at the Neches River settlement. In the summer of 1835 three merchants—Henry Millard, Joseph Pulsifer, and Thomas Huling—opened a store in the town of Santa Anna. Millard bought fifty acres of land from Noah Tevis for a new townsite, just to the north of Santa Anna, and named it Beaumont. After the Texas Revolution, the three men, as partners in J. P. Pulsifer and Company, added fifty acres to the original purchase and took as additional partners Nancy Tevis, Noah Tevis's widow (Noah had died in 1835), and Joseph Grigsby, another early settler. Each of the new partners contributed fifty acres, increasing the overall size of the townsite to two hundred acres. The new town of Beaumont eventually absorbed the two earlier settlements.[4]

Both James and Elizabeth McFaddin left their mark on early records of the town. Strong and independent, neither hesitated to follow an unconventional course of action if the occasion warranted it. While living at Moss Bluff, James had refused to join a group of settlers who opposed an unpopular Mexican garrison commander, incurring the resentment of many of them and possibly influencing his decision to leave.[5] Later, as a resident of Jefferson County, he was fined ten dollars for interrupting a meeting of the Jefferson County Court.[6]

Even in frontier Texas, where a certain amount of independence was necessary for women to survive, Elizabeth was unusual. In 1835, she proposed to rent her house to Beaumont's first schoolteacher, indicating an interest in education as well as a head for business.[7] In 1838 she and her husband signed an agreement that provided her with specified amounts of land, cash, and livestock in case she "legally demanded" a divorce. Later she contracted alone to build a house.[8] She is listed in the 1840 Texas census as one of only eight female landowners in Jefferson County.[9]

During their marriage, James and Elizabeth McFaddin had four children: William, born in 1819; David, 1821; Eliza, 1822; and Sarah, about 1829. William joined the Texian army during the Texas Revolution. He was at the Battle of Bexar in late 1835, where he suffered from frostbite, and later joined Sam Houston on his long retreat across Texas. During the Battle of San Jacinto he was assigned to guard the baggage and the soldiers who had been wounded.[10] In a letter to his father dated May 4, 1836, William proudly wrote:

> I have the great satisfaction to inform you that we have
> had a most glorious battle with the Mexicans and have
> given them a shameful whipping. . . .

And later in the letter:

> I do not want you to be in any ways uneasy about me nor
> look for me until you see me as I intend to stay in the army
> until my time is up and get an honorable discharge with the
> rest of the company.[11]

William was discharged at Goliad on June 8, 1836, his seventeenth birthday, and, according to family tradition, walked all the way home to Beaumont, a distance of several hundred miles.[12] When the Republic of Texas granted him the land that he was entitled to, both as a settler and as a participant in the Battle of San Jacinto, he located his

177-acre labor just west of his father's survey and just north of the Noah Tevis survey.

In 1838 William married Rachel Williams, daughter of pioneers Hezekiah and Nancy Reams Williams, who had settled in the Beaumont area in 1834. William and Rachel had nine children: James A., born in 1840; John Andrew, 1844; Sarah L., 1846; David H., 1847; Druzilla, 1849; Eliza Ann (Di), 1851; William Perry Herring, 1856; Charles Walter, 1859; and Elizabeth (Lizzie), 1862.[13]

While William and Rachel's children were growing up, Beaumont became a thriving community, both under the Republic of Texas and, after 1845, as part of the state of Texas. Most of Beaumont's citizens were in agriculture-related occupations; cattle raising became the area's first industry. Open prairie, including the McFaddin lands, lay west and south of Beaumont, and the McFaddins and other early ranchers began to amass large herds of cattle, which they periodically drove east on the Atascosito Trail to the New Orleans market.[14]

James McFaddin died in 1845, his wife Elizabeth in 1846. Their son William carried on the family business of raising cattle and at the same time began increasing his land holdings. In 1853 he bought 45 $1/2$ acres out of the original Noah Tevis survey that lay along the Atascosito Trail, known by then as the Liberty Road.[15] (This land, which adjoined his survey immediately to the south, is where the McFaddin-Ward House stands today; the carriage house is on the original William McFaddin survey. North Street, which separates the main house from the carriage house, runs along the boundary of the two surveys.)[16]

Because of its location on the Neches River and the Liberty Road, Beaumont became an important supply center at the beginning of the Civil War in 1861. William McFaddin, after serving seven months as captain of Patrol District No. 1, became an official supplier of beef to the Confederate Army. He obtained a ferry license so he could swim his cattle across the Neches River at a designated spot (afterward called McFaddin's Crossing) without paying regular ferry fees.[17] In 1863, the same year that the Confederate forces won the Battle of Sabine Pass, William's son John Andrew McFaddin died at the Battle of Fordoche Bayou, Louisiana.[18]

The Civil War did not destroy the Texas economy as it did that of the Deep South, nor was Reconstruction in Texas the long, painful process it was in other states. Beaumont began to rebuild relatively

William McFaddin, 1893.

quickly. From the earliest years, a fledgling lumber industry had existed; cypress trees were cut in the river bottoms, floated downstream to the town, and hand-fashioned into cypress shingles to be exported to Galveston or New Orleans. By the 1850s, steam sawmills had been installed along the river and were producing boards and beams from the plentiful pine and hardwood, ready to be shipped out on the early steamboats or railroads. The postwar era saw a tremendous growth in the lumber industry, and with it came even more steamboats and railroads to export the finished products. Beaumont became a prosperous lumber town.[19]

During this era of growth and prosperity William Perry Herring (WPH) McFaddin came of age. Although his father William had himself lacked a formal education, he saw to it that his children received as much schooling as possible. As a boy W. P. H. McFaddin

Rachel McFaddin, ca. 1893. Married at sixteen, she bore
nine children, the last at the age of forty-one.

was instructed by teachers who lived in the McFaddin home. Later, he
attended Texas Military Institute in Austin and Jones Commercial
College in St. Louis, Missouri. At the age of seventeen he took over
William's stockraising business.[20]

William himself was reportedly a man of prodigious energy, a man
who credited his success to the fact that he got up "earlier than
everyone else."[21] He passed on this attribute to his son WPH, who
could work all day on his ranch, dance that night until the wee hours,
and get up before sunup the next morning to work another full day.
Another trait W. P. H. McFaddin inherited from his father was a
lifelong passion for land, and like his father he spent a lifetime amass-
ing a territorial empire. It was said of WPH that he did not want much
land—only what was his, and what was next to it.

In the years before the turn of the century, father and son continued

Emma Janes McFaddin, ca. 1887. She was only thirty-four
when she died in 1890 of a "congestive chill." *Courtesy Grace
Cordts.*

to increase their land holdings, their transactions filling the record
books at the Jefferson County Courthouse. Together they also worked
steadily to expand an already-flourishing cattle concern. In addition,
WPH began to diversify the family's interests, which eventually came
to include rice farming and milling, meat packing, fur trapping, and
commercial real estate.

During this time the two men began their association with Dr.
Obadiah Kyle and Valentine Wiess, husbands of William's nieces,
Helen and Mary Elizabeth Herring. In 1888 the McFaddin-Wiess-Kyle
partnership formed the Beaumont Pasture Company to utilize for
grazing the vast coastal prairies that it had accumulated in south
Jefferson County. The partnership also formed the McFaddin-Wiess-

The children of W. P. H. and Emma Janes McFaddin, ca. 1887: Di Vernon, Skipwith, and Val. *Courtesy Grace Cordts.*

Kyle Rice Mill, the McFaddin-Wiess-Kyle Irrigation Company, and other business enterprises.[22]

Sometime around 1877 WPH married Emma Janes, a member of another pioneer Beaumont family. They had three children, Lillian Skipwith, born in 1877; DiVernon, 1879; and William Valentine, 1883. WPH and Emma settled in a house in what was then the western outskirts of Beaumont, not far from his father's land.[23]

Two of William's other sons, James A. and David H., moved to Victoria, Texas, and built a ranching empire. (David was reputed to be six feet, seven inches tall, whereas WPH, only five feet, eleven inches tall, was considered the runt of the family.) William's four daughters, Sarah Alexander, Druzilla Kent, Elizabeth (Lizzie) Coward, and Eliza

Ida Caldwell McFaddin's wedding portrait, 1894. She purchased her wedding attire in Cincinnati; the gown was custom-made by her favorite dressmaker, Anna Dunlevy.

W. P. H. McFaddin's wedding portrait, 1894.

Ann (Di), who married W. C. Averill, settled in the Beaumont area. Charles, WPH's younger brother, lived in Beaumont for a time but later moved away.[24]

By the 1890s the lumber industry had reached its zenith in Beaumont, supplying distant markets using the complex network of railroads that connected the town to the rest of the world. Wealthy lumber barons infused the town with new money and energy, transforming Beaumont from a frontier settlement into a fast-growing little town. It still contained many unrefined elements, such as lumber stacked along the streets, livestock roaming freely downtown, and an overabundance of saloons. But it also had a fine hotel (the Crosby House), an opera house, a water system (then used only for firefighting), a telephone switchboard, and electric lighting. Gracious Victorian mansions, constructed of the finest lumber, went up in the fashionable areas of town.[25]

Emma McFaddin died suddenly in 1890, leaving WPH a widower with three young children.[26] In 1893 he met Ida Regina Caldwell of Huntington, West Virginia. Ida, born in 1872, was the daughter of wealthy businessman, railroad and coal magnate James Lewis Caldwell and his wife, Mary O'Bannon Smith Caldwell. She had come to Beaumont to visit Sadie Caswell, a classmate at Mary Baldwin Seminary in Staunton, Virginia. Ida hoped also to alleviate a slight respiratory problem, as her doctor had prescribed a stay in a hot, dry place. (Apparently neither of them were familiar with the humid climate of southeast Texas). At first unhappy with some of the less elegant aspects of Beaumont, such as the lack of indoor plumbing, she was soon enjoying herself at social activities. Eventually she met W. P. H. McFaddin, and they fell in love.[27] He wrote her father for permission to marry her, and Mr. Caldwell responded:

> I not only desire but fully rely on my daughter's ability to choose a husband for herself. . . . I have no doubt of your devotion to her and hers to you. She is . . . willing to place her life to your keeping and being assured by both you and her of your devotions to each other I feel it my duty to submit to the choice of my darling child.[28]

On December 4, 1894, WPH and Ida were married in Huntington. After an extended honeymoon in the eastern United States, they returned to Beaumont to live.[29]

The children of W. P. H. and Ida McFaddin, ca. 1907: Perry, Caldwell, and Mamie. Holding Caldwell is Minnie Burke Curley, Ida's lifelong friend and Mamie's godmother.

Only five years older than WPH's oldest daughter Skip, Ida nevertheless established a good relationship with her stepchildren, who called her "Sister Ida," or "Stida." Soon she and WPH began to add children to the brood: Mamie Louise, born in 1895; William Perry Herring, Jr. (known as Perry), 1897; and James Lewis Caldwell (known as Caldwell), 1901.

The marriage of W. P. H. and Ida McFaddin represented a turning point in the life-style of the McFaddin family. William and Rachel, though quite prosperous, had nevertheless remained hardworking pioneers, products of the Texas frontier. Likewise, WPH had lived with his first wife in a modest, albeit comfortable, home. Ida, however, imbued all her activities with her own distinctive style, altering the lives of her new family and making an indelible impression on Beaumont society. A true grande dame, she was elegant and sophisticated, surrounding herself with fine things, from her fashionable clothing to her beautifully appointed home. She soon took the lead, not only in society, but also in civic and charitable work, giving full rein to her strong sense of noblesse oblige and her natural aptitude for leadership and organization.

William McFaddin died in 1897, his wife Rachel in 1898. The home they had built on Tevis land went to their daughter Di and her husband, W. C. Averill. The surrounding land was parceled out among all of William and Rachel's children.[30] As the city continued to grow, the acreage where William had grazed cattle was divided into residential lots and blocks, called the McFaddin Addition and later the Averill Addition.[31]

Beaumont's population steadily increased during the last decade of the nineteenth century; in the first part of the twentieth, it took a giant leap. In 1901 the economies of Beaumont and the world were changed forever when the Lucas Gusher blew in on Spindletop Hill. The town of 9,000 for a time was forced to accommodate 50,000 as people flocked in to sightsee and make their fortunes. By the end of the year, the population had stabilized at 20,000 and the town had acquired a new economic base—petroleum.[32]

The fortunes of the McFaddins were enhanced and diversified by the discovery, as the well had been drilled on land owned by the Beaumont Pasture Company.[33] In addition, as the fashionable Calder Avenue neighborhood continued to grow to the west, the land in the Averill Addition, owned by William McFaddin's heirs, increased greatly in value.

2.
THE HOUSE

THE FRAME HOUSE in which W. P. H. and Ida McFaddin lived right after their marriage in 1894 was located on Liberty Avenue, in the Calder Avenue neighborhood. WPH had probably been living in this house with the three children from his previous marriage. Ida's arrival, however, brought many changes to the family's life-style, one of which was the house in which they lived.

A modest, one-story frame house could hardly have seemed suitable to a young woman from a wealthy West Virginia family who was accustomed to fine surroundings. Moving to a relatively small Texas town required adjustment enough, and Ida, independent and intelligent, was not about to remain a passive observer. Instead, she set about creating an atmosphere in which she could be happy and comfortable. It was undoubtedly her presence and influence that brought about the construction of the family's next house.

This house, built in 1896, was, like the widely known W. H. Stark house built in 1894 in nearby Orange, typical of late Victorian architecture. A Queen Anne style house, designed by D. P. Kaufman & Company Architects, it blended well with the other fashionable houses on Calder Avenue. The McFaddins hired local contractor P. J. Connolly to build the house at a cost of $5,265.[1] Upon its completion, a Beaumont newspaper reported that the new house was "complete in the minutest appointment" and complimented Ida on her decorating acumen.[2] Inside and out, the house was architecturally in step with its time. And its Victorian conglomeration of furnishings, as illustrated in contemporary interior photographs, was evidence of the family's mainstream decorating tastes.

McFaddin home on Liberty Avenue, February 1895. The occasion for the photograph was a rare snowstorm in Beaumont.

By the end of the Victorian age, however, Queen Anne architecture was giving way to more symmetrical, classically inspired designs. Therefore, in 1906, when the McFaddins had the opportunity to acquire the house WPH's sister and brother-in-law Di and W. C. Averill were building, they did so. The Averills had needed a new house because the one they had been living in, the original William McFaddin home built in 1859, had burned in 1905. The fire destroyed everything except the night clothes the residents were wearing and a few small items they grabbed on their way out of the burning home. But the Averills had carried insurance on the furnishings and house, which a local newspaper called "one of the most picturesque and handsomely furnished in the city," and soon set out to build a new home of similar grandeur.[3]

The exact reasons for the Averills' decision to give up their new home are unclear, but the general consensus is that they decided the house was too large for their needs. It was just fine, though, for W. P. H. and Ida McFaddin and their children. They traded their house and land on Calder Avenue, plus $30,000 in cash, to the Averills for the new house and the entire block of land on which it was built. In a

McFaddin home at 1316 Calder Avenue, ca. 1896. This house is no longer standing.

Drawing room, 1316 Calder Avenue, ca. 1900. The interiors of the public rooms in the McFaddins' Calder Avenue home are well documented by two sets of photographs made between 1896 and 1906.

separate transaction, in exchange for ten dollars and several lots of land, the Averills also sold the McFaddins a parcel of land on the block behind the house, where the McFaddins eventually built a carriage house. Thus, the Averills moved into the McFaddins' ten-year-old Calder Avenue house, while in January 1907 the McFaddins moved into the new Beaux-Arts Colonial house at 1906 McFaddin Avenue.[4]

To design and oversee construction of the house, the Averills had commissioned local architect Henry Conrad Mauer (1873–1939). A native of LaGrange, Texas, Mauer had moved to Beaumont in 1901, shortly after the discovery of oil at Spindletop, and set up his own firm in 1903. His career was noted for a number of significant local structures, including private residences, schools, fire stations, and commercial buildings. A student at the Pratt Institute in Brooklyn, New York, he had received his Certificate in Architecture in 1898 after two years of study.[5] In addition to courses in basic architectural principles, he would have been exposed to modern trends in architectural design. Among these trends was the Beaux-Arts style, influenced largely by the classical architecture of ancient Greece and Rome and promoted

William McFaddin/W. C. Averill house, 1901. The burning of this house in 1905 (then occupied by the W.C. Averills) led to the construction of what is today the McFaddin-Ward House. According to newspaper reports, an extensive collection of magazines and rare books and a table inlaid with gold were among the many possessions destroyed. *Art Souvenir of Beaumont, Texas, 1901* (Beaumont: George W. Carroll et al., 1901). *Courtesy Tyrrell Historical Library.*

McFaddin home at 1906 McFaddin Avenue, as published in *Southern Orchards and Homes* in 1909. The building in the background is the carriage house.

by the École des Beaux Arts in Paris. Growing interest in early America also had an impact on architectural design. Elements of these and other styles could be seen in an increasing number of buildings, especially those exhibited at world's fairs and expositions, and it is no surprise that a grand home designed by a professionally trained, aspiring young architect should exhibit characteristics of the latest styles.

Mauer combined the Beaux-Arts features of the house—the colossal-order portico, elegant proportions, and classically inspired, applied ornamentation—with standard elements of colonial revival architecture, such as a Georgian floor plan with central hall. The result was an early and important example of colonial revival architecture in Texas. The Centennial Exposition of 1876 had created widespread interest in America's colonial years, and in the years following the exposition forms and motifs prevalent during the country's colonial and early republic years increasingly influenced architectural, as well as decorative arts, designs. (Georgian elements usually characterized mid-eighteenth-century colonial architecture, while neoclassical styles prevailed during the Federal period, from circa 1780 to circa 1820.) Colonial revival designs were not, at least at the beginning of the movement, intended to be exact copies, but the colonial influence was obvious, evoking a strong sense of nostalgia in a people newly conscious of their heritage.[6] Grand Texas homes besides the McFaddins', such as Amarillo's Harrington house (built in 1914), Fort Worth's Thistle Hill (built in 1903), and Wichita Falls' Kell house (built in 1909), exhibit other interpretations of the colonial and classical revival styles.

By combining elements of colonial revival architecture with those of the Beaux-Arts style, architects like Mauer were attempting to infuse the traditional with the modern and thus create a new, enduring, American style of architecture.[7] A Houston magazine, *Southern Orchards and Homes*, featured the McFaddins' house in its February 1909 issue and explained Mauer's design approach: "In designing this beautiful mansion, it was the intention of the architect to first consider proportions; second, simplicity; and third, harmony." The stylistic combination of these three principles made the structure vastly different from popular architectural styles of just a few years earlier. And people liked it. The *Southern Orchards and Homes* article reflected popular reaction by saying that "the building stands today to show for itself its architectural beauty and as one of the best in Texas."[8]

While the house did receive plenty of attention when it was built, it was by no means the only example of its type. Similar, though not identical, examples were built in cities and towns throughout Texas in the first decade of the twentieth century. But the style could be found elsewhere, too. Buildings, such as the Buckner house (current home to the Saline County Historical Society) built in Marshall, Missouri, in 1906, and the North Carolina State Building exhibited at the 1907 Jamestown Exposition, bore close resemblance. While the McFaddins' home may have been built on a grander scale than many of the similar buildings, its design was merely based upon one set of architectural philosophies and characteristics popular at the time.

Construction, performed by day laborers, began in August 1905, and on October 25 the Beaumont *Enterprise* ran its own celebratory article about Mauer's design. A "handsome pen picture," it explained, displayed in a window of a local jewelry store (in the same building as Mauer's office), evoked great excitement, not only because of the design, but also because of the young architect's general success in the

Postcard illustration of the North Carolina State Building at the Jamestown Exposition, 1907.

town. According to the *Enterprise*, Mauer won the Averill commission over "one of the acknowledged great architects of the south."[9] This architect was probably George Barber, who had designed Beaumont's J. F. Keith home (1902) and Ed Carroll home (1901–1902). He also supplied the drawings for the L. Parish house (circa 1893) in Calvert, Texas, and for many others throughout the United States. This was possible because Barber based his career on mail-order architecture and was indeed a well-known, highly respected architect. By the time the Keith and Carroll houses were built, he was headquartered in Knoxville, Tennessee.[10]

In addition to three full stories, Mauer also included in his design of the 12,800-square-foot house a one-room fourth floor and, unusual in the Gulf Coast region, a half basement to contain the boiler, coal bin, and laundry sinks. To construct cement walks in the yard and around the entire block (about 1,500 feet in all), Averill hired the Beaumont Construction Company in what the newpaper described as "one of the largest cement sidewalk contracts let in some time."[11] The house was not quite finished when the Averills moved in during 1906, so (according to family tradition) they settled in on the third floor, which was finished first, for the few months that they actually resided there. The other areas of which they made notable use before moving out were the parlor, where their niece Kydie Coward married Norval McKee in January 1907, and other first-floor rooms needed for the occasion.[12] The McFaddins moved in shortly after the wedding.

Mauer's plan exhibits a combination of original design elements and mail-order components, with local and area materials and labor extensively used. The exterior wooden elements are largely cypress, from the Bettis Manufacturing Company in Beaumont, and native yellow pine. Inside, hardwoods, primarily oak, predominate. The Diana Brick and Tile Manufacturing Company of nearby Loeb, Texas, produced most of the brick used in the structure. The large, medieval-inspired fireplace in the entrance hall was, however, apparently built from a kit for "Elizabethan Mantels" ordered from a company in Boston.[13]

Many other interior architectural elements were more than likely also mail-order products. The McFaddins needed just a little bit more room, so immediately after moving in they hired Mauer to design a breakfast room to be added to the northeast corner of the house. Invoices and correspondence indicate that ready-made features, such as columns, paneling, stained glass, oak flooring, and light fixtures were ordered and brought in by rail from the Lecoutour Brothers Stair Manufacturing Company of St. Louis. Similar details in other rooms suggest mail-order origins, as well.

In addition to aesthetic appeal, Mauer's design emphasized comfort. The region's hot, muggy climate presented special challenges to architects working in the pre-air-conditioning age. To counteract such problems, Mauer pointed the building to the south and gave most rooms an exterior opening toward the same direction, thus taking advantage of prevailing breezes. High ceilings, ceiling fans, transomed doors, and double-sash windows also contributed to ventilation in the house. Additionally, there were porches on each level. On the first floor, the shaded, wide porch initially wrapped around the entire front portion of the building. Such design elements, included to ease life in a hot climate, were often central to architecture throughout the south, and a turn-of-the-century style designation for structures like the McFaddins' was simply "Southern Colonial."[14]

For the cool days of winter, a steam heating system was installed as a part of the original plan to heat the first floor. Gas logs in the entrance hall and parlor helped, but their function was also decorative. (The original gas logs are still in place.) On the second floor, the wood-burning fireplaces were the main source of heat until the 1920s, when radiators were added there.[15] The fireplaces themselves gradually became less valuable as heating devices, but their decorative significance continues. Each one is different in design and represents contemporary tastes ranging from Arts and Crafts themes (dining room) to the neoclassical (parlor). One need only look at the fireplace to determine the original character and decorative nature of the room.

Needless to say, the house incorporated many modern conveniences. One of the most important features was that it was fully electrified when built. The original knob-and-tube system still exists and functions, and push-button switches continue to operate light fixtures (though new wiring was installed to accommodate added electrical demands, such as those created by the climate control system). Plumbing, also a modern feature in 1906, was used extensively in the house. Five baths (one on the first floor, three on the second, and one on the third) were part of the original plan. Two more were added on the second floor in 1912, so each bedroom on that floor had its own bath. As a result of the fire that destroyed the William McFaddin home, all three floors were equipped with a standpipe and hose system for fire protection.

Despite the modern technology in the house, servants were still a key aspect of household operations. An interior telephone system, with extensions located in the master and pink bedrooms, the kitchen, the first floor hallway beneath the stairs, and the carriage house, made it possible to contact servants in various parts of the complex. For summoning servants in the kitchen, call buttons in rooms throughout the house were connected to a box in the kitchen. When a button was pushed, an arrow flipped up, indicating to the servants the room from which the call was coming. The master and pink bedrooms were each equipped with yet another button used to call servants when they were not in the kitchen area.

At the beginning of the twentieth century, domestic servants still often lived at the house where they were employed. The McFaddins' carriage house, in the block behind the main house, contained the quarters for the family's servants. The building, probably constructed shortly after the land came into WPH's possession, also had a garage (originally intended for carriages), a stable, a hayloft above the stable,

Ida McFaddin and her chickens, ca. 1911. The building on the right is the carriage house.

and a gymnasium. The grounds on the west side of the building served for a time as a lot for horses and cows.[16] And Ida McFaddin's chicken coops were located behind the carriage house on the north side. As an amateur, she raised chickens for several years, a popular hobby taken up by women all over the country early in the twentieth century. She must have been fairly successful, for in a letter dated March 6, 1911, ten-year-old Caldwell practically shouted to his sister, who was away at school, "The Incubator has hached [sic] and we got 25 little chicks."[17]

The carriage house exhibits stylistic features similar to those of its parent building. A white, classically inspired, two-story structure, it measures about 8,000 square feet. It was built at the time automobiles were becoming more commonplace in America. The McFaddins bought their first one, a sixteen-horsepower Mitchell touring car, in 1907, but they also continued to rely on horse-powered transportation for a while.[18] Fronting on North Street (the northern boundary of the McFaddin-Ward House block), the carriage house was located so that carriages or cars could pull out of the garage, enter the main house lot on the driveway right across the street, and pull up under the *porte cochere* at the west side of the house.

While the carriage house essentially retains its original appearance, a few notable alterations were made to the main residence. Most occurred in the house's early years and did not significantly change its exterior appearance. One of the first major changes was the addition of the breakfast room in 1907. That same year, a bedroom was added at the north end of the second floor, presumably for the McFaddins' two little boys, whose mother wanted their room near hers. A milk room and a lock room (for bulk storage of food items) were added off the back porch.[19]

Other changes followed in the next few decades. Kitchen remodeling led to the expansion of the butler's pantry, the removal of a freight elevator, and the addition of a large storage pantry in 1912. This was also when the two new bathrooms were added, and the second-floor front porch area was screened and fitted up as a sleeping porch.[20] This latter change corresponded with a national trend toward healthful living, which advocates said could be enhanced by sleeping outdoors and breathing fresh air. One architect even contended, "The secret is

Breakfast room, 1909.

that you breathe the fresh pure air during your sleeping hours, which is worth more than any apothecary's pills in the world."[21] About ten years later, the McFaddins enclosed the east side of their front porch on the first floor and made it into a sun porch.[22] This room was used as a summer sitting room for many years.

The absence of major structural alterations to the house enhances its usefulness as a record of early twentieth-century design. But more than just an architectural record, the house reveals a way of life and represents an era in Beaumont's history when building this sort of house was not a bit unusual. It is one of only a few of its type still standing in the town, and thanks to an abundance of available information, much is known about the family and its life in the house.

3.
LIFE-STYLES AND COMMUNITY

WHEN W. P. H. AND IDA MCFADDIN moved into their new home, Beaumonters were still enjoying the prosperity that had begun in the days of the lumber boom. Beaumont boasted a strong, diverse economy, based on lumber, cattle, rice, and petroleum. Even the gradual diminution of the Spindletop oil field held no fears, for the construction of the Magnolia refinery and other oil-related industries had ensured the city's future as a petroleum processing center.

The railroads, which had supplanted the riverboats in transporting goods to and from the East Texas interior, made up a vast network connecting Beaumont with the rest of the country. In 1908 Beaumonters realized their long-held dream of a deepwater port for their city when a channel was dug in the Neches River, joining Beaumont with the Port Arthur ship channel. The city thus became a major shipping center.

Spindletop had generated a construction boom, bringing the downtown area a number of modern buildings, such as a new post office, fire station, and Baptist church, and several significant modern improvements, such as natural gas lines and an artesian water supply.[1] New homes went up all over town, and soon the Averill Addition was a pleasant neighborhood containing a number of large, expensive homes.

W. P. H. McFaddin's new home was one of the largest of these. The ground floor of the house was made for entertaining, and Ida McFaddin took full advantage of this feature. Hardly a week passed without some mention in the Beaumont society column of a luncheon,

Mamie McFaddin and friends in her friend Leonora Norvell's car, ca. 1912. Mamie is the second from the right.

card club, musicale, porch dance, or other gathering at the "palatial home" of Mr. and Mrs. W. P. H. McFaddin. Even Mamie, Perry, and Caldwell—ages eleven, ten, and six, respectively, when they moved into the house—had their own entertainment. When they were small, Ida gave them birthday and other holiday parties on the lawn. As teenagers and young adults, they held dances on the broad front porch. On several occasions Mamie invited her finishing school friends to a "house party" to stay at her home for several days.[2] (WPH's two oldest children never lived in the house, and Val married and moved out in 1908.)

A house the size of the McFaddins' required a full staff of servants to keep it going. Over the years, some of the servants lived in the carriage house and on the grounds, while others lived elsewhere in town. The number of servants employed by the McFaddins varied, with the maximum at eight: butler, upstairs maid, downstairs maid, cook, laundress, yard man, chauffeur for W. P. H. McFaddin, and chauffeur for Ida Caldwell McFaddin.[3]

Neither Ida nor W. P. H. McFaddin ever learned to drive. Family tradition holds that WPH, on his maiden driving expedition, unthinkingly tried to stop the car by shouting "whoa," and it ran halfway up the post office steps before finally stalling. Ida, who was with him, announced in definite tones that she did not know how he intended to get home, but she was going to take the street car. The ultimate result was that each maintained an automobile and hired a chauffeur. Mamie, however, received her first car in 1912 and usually drove herself about.[4]

Mamie, Perry, and Caldwell grew to adulthood in the house on McFaddin Avenue. Mamie first attended Bell Austin Institute, a private grade school in Beaumont, then studied at Gunston Hall, a finishing school in Washington, D.C. Perry and Caldwell attended Bell Austin and Beaumont High School, then went on to Rice Institute (now Rice University) in Houston. Perry also served a short stint in the army during World War I, and Caldwell graduated from Harvard Law School.

After the boys finished their educations, they joined WPH in business. Although Caldwell initially practiced law for several years, he eventually took over administration of the McFaddin family business affairs, while Perry took over the ranching end.[5] In 1925 Caldwell married Rosine Blount of Nacogdoches, Texas, and in 1926 Perry married Amizetta Northcott White of Huntington, West Virginia. Both sons built homes near their parents, in a neighborhood that continued to grow and expand with young families. Eventually it extended all the way to Eleventh Street, which in turn became one of Beaumont's major thoroughfares.

Mamie returned home from Gunston Hall at the end of the 1912 school year and settled into a very active Beaumont society as one of its reigning belles. She attended parties, dances, and luncheons, shopped or traveled with her mother, and visited friends. About 1913, she also began to date Carroll Ward.[6]

Carroll, son of John C. and Belle Carroll Ward, was the seventh of eleven children.[7] His father, a prosperous local businessman, bought the first car in Jefferson County in 1900.[8] Carroll was a gifted athlete; although not a large man, he was quick and tenacious. He played football at Baylor University in 1907, then at Texas A&M in 1909 and 1910. At A&M he was chosen for the 1909 all-conference team and later

Mamie McFaddin, 1911, in the conservatory. To describe the photograph, she wrote, "I was sixteen years old and led the Grand March with Lynn Gilbert for the Thanksgiving Dance."

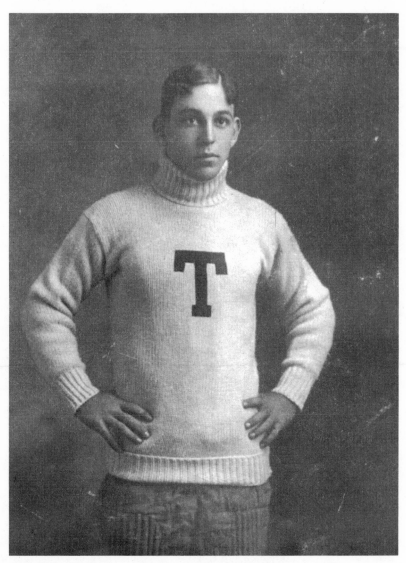

Carroll Ward in Texas A&M uniform, 1909 or 1910. At the time, A&M was a branch of the University of Texas, hence the "T" on the sweater. In 1984 Carroll was named to the Texas A&M Football Hall of Fame.

named one of the school's all-time great left ends. At this time he received the nickname "Doggie."[9]

After the 1910 football season, Carroll returned to Beaumont and went to work in the Ward family business, the Texas Ice Company. During World War I, he joined the army and received training as a pilot. When he and Mamie McFaddin began dating, W. P. H. and Ida McFaddin were said to have objected because of Carroll's wild reputation. Mamie and Carroll continued to see each other, however, and on May 21, 1919, two months after he received his discharge from the army, the couple was married in the parlor of the McFaddin home in what one newspaper called "a brilliant social affair." After an extended honeymoon trip to Cincinnati and Huntington, they returned to live with her parents at 1906 McFaddin Avenue. Once married, Carroll was apparently able to subdue his wild streak. For a short while he worked for his father-in-law, managing the McFaddin muskrat fur business, but soon returned to the Texas Ice Company.[10]

Mamie and Carroll Ward were different in many ways—her immaculate appearance and emphasis on etiquette and tradition, his khakis and boots and casual manner. Yet they formed a lifelong bond which to all appearances was a happy one. They went to movies, ate out, attended vaudeville shows, fairs, masquerade parties, dances, A&M football games, and wrestling matches, and at times even played golf or miniature golf together. If they had nothing else planned, they would ride around in their car in the evenings to visit friends or relatives or merely to take in the air.

As a young wife, Mamie quickly established a place for herself in the household routine. When she married, her mother turned over some of the household operations to her; Mamie oversaw much of the daily cleaning and meal preparation, as well as seasonal cleaning and repairs. To spare her mother the disruption of major projects, she tried to schedule them for when her mother was out of town. Mamie accepted these duties as a lifetime commitment and assigned them priority over nearly everything but her family. Her brother Caldwell referred to his childhood home as a "woman killer" because of the amount of work required to maintain it.[11]

Everyday life at the McFaddins' home followed a fairly well-established routine. WPH and Carroll rose early in the morning, often at four or five, taking a hearty meal in the breakfast room before heading to their respective business interests. Not wanting to get up so early, the women eventually developed a better system. They began their daily routines by having servants serve them breakfast in their rooms. After eating, they bathed and performed their morning facial ritual—cleansing cream, padded wand for toning facial muscles, astringent, ice to close pores, and finally moisturizing lotion, rouge, powder, and lipstick. Then they fixed their hair for the day. Thus fortified, they issued the day's instructions to the servants: menu to the cook; cleaning and work schedule to the maids, butler, and yard man; travel plans for the day to the chauffeur.

If they were to spend the morning at home, Ida and Mamie dressed in cotton dresses (called "wash dresses"). A popular at-home pastime was to telephone friends and exchange the latest news. Other activities were sewing (usually handwork), reading, supervising housecleaning, corresponding, planning social or organizational affairs, or resting. Often in the afternoon the women took a nap on their daybeds, then later rose and dressed to receive callers. If the ladies had a luncheon, tea, meeting, or other function to attend, or wished to go shopping, they put on an appropriate dress or suit, complete with hat and gloves.

In good weather Ida and Mamie often devoted the late afternoon to porch sitting or driving about. Evening was reserved for dinner and usually for other activities that included their husbands. At bedtime both women performed another facial ritual and took another bath. In the summer they sometimes took as many as three or four baths a day, one way of surviving Beaumont's hot summer weather.[12]

Another way to cope with the heat, particularly among the wealthier classes, was simply to leave town. Every year, when the children were young, Ida took them to Huntington to visit her relatives. One summer the family went to Michigan and another they spent in Maine. The McFaddins also owned a beach house at Caplen, on the Bolivar Peninsula, where they could stay relatively cool. After the beach house was destroyed in the 1915 hurricane that struck Galveston, Ida rented a home at Winslow, Arkansas, a resort area in the Ozarks, where she could enjoy the cool mountain air. She canned blackberries, made huckleberry jelly, and socialized with other vacationers, while the children picnicked and played golf and tennis. In 1930 the family rebuilt at Caplen, this time three houses—one for Perry, one for

Caldwell, and one for Ida, WPH, Mamie, and Carroll—and resumed summer life at the beach. The new beach homes did not prevent the McFaddins from traveling to more distant places, however. In 1933 Ida and a friend went to Europe, and in 1938, she and Mamie went on a second European trek.[13]

In spite of their enjoyment of the trappings of wealth, neither Ida nor Mamie was idle. Ida had talents that in a later day would have served her well in a corporate career: creativity, organizational skills, and the ability to motivate people. Her gracious manner assured her the willing cooperation of employees and associates alike. In a few cases, she actually delved into traditionally masculine realms. After the deaths of her brothers, she served capably as president of the J. L. Caldwell Company, the company her father had founded in Huntington. She also stayed abreast of her husband's business affairs, offering him advice and encouragement.[14]

As befitted a lady of means in those times, however, Ida utilized most of her talents in volunteer activities. She combined an active social consciousness with innovative, even daring ideas. One particularly successful effort, to benefit the pew fund at St. Mark's Episcopal Church, was held in 1900 at the Jefferson County Courthouse, where she staged a mock divorce trial between herself and W. P. H. McFaddin. The novelty brought extensive publicity, as well as a packed house, to the cause.[15]

She was active in St. Mark's Episcopal Church as a Guild member, Sunday School teacher, and member of the choir. In both world wars she headed up the Red Cross volunteer effort, supervising the making of bandages, blankets, and other items. She served on the board of the Beaumont Children's Home, belonged to the Women's Club, and helped to organize the Beaumont United Charities (later United Way). Numerous other organizations benefited from her generosity. She was most active in the Daughters of the American Revolution, serving first as state regent (1931–1934), then vice president general of the national society (1934–1937). Her travels throughout Texas to organize new D.A.R. chapters, in a chauffeur-driven lavender Pierce-Arrow, made her something of a legend in her time.[16]

Mamie was much like her mother, both in her enjoyment of the finer things of life and her penchant for community service. During Ida's lifetime, however, Mamie generally allowed her mother to take

Ida Caldwell McFaddin, ca. 1930.

the lead, assisting her in activities such as the Red Cross and Beaumont Children's Home. Two exceptions to this trait were her involvement in the Magnolia Garden Club and in the National Society of the Colonial Dames of America in the State of Texas. In these organizations, Mamie was actually more active than her mother. At the Garden Club's founding in 1937, Mamie was elected vice president and continued to be active in its leadership; she served the Colonial Dames as a member of the state board.[17]

Along with her many other activities, Ida kept the home fires burning, while her husband's sights were focused on his numerous business interests. With his enormous energy, W. P. H. McFaddin was able to remain active into old age, dividing his time among his office in downtown Beaumont, his ranch in south Jefferson County, and his ranch in Knox County in northern Texas. He rarely took the summer-long vacations planned by the rest of his family, preferring instead to join them occasionally for a few days when his schedule allowed. He was active in various organizations, primarily business oriented, such as the Coastal Cattlemen's Association, the Good Roads Association, and the Concatenated Order of Hoo Hoo (an international social organization for lumbermen). He was also a director of the First National Bank in Beaumont.

However diverse his interests, WPH never lost his love for his ranchland. A cattleman born and bred, he could ride his horse with the ranch hands all day long, even in his old age. People who knew him recall seeing him on horseback, with reins in one hand, and in the other hand an umbrella to protect against the sun. When he did allow his chauffeur, Tom Parker, to drive him about on the ranch, he would become angry because Tom refused to leave the road and drive cross country as though they were on horseback.[18] Not long before his death at the age of seventy-nine, he struck out across his ranch on a horse commandeered from a ranch hand and, when night fell, lost his bearings. He was found just before dawn the next morning, none the worse for his wanderings, and denied that he had ever been lost: "I'm on my own ranch, ain't I?"[19]

Some who knew W. P. H. McFaddin considered him a gruff, even hard, man. Certainly he was outspoken. In 1912 he wrote a letter to the Beaumont *Enterprise* headed "Why Cost of Living Is High," stating his belief that the shortness of the modern workday was one factor in

W. P. H. McFaddin and cowhand Jack Frank branding calves, ca. 1920. Typically, he is wearing white shirt, vest, and tie, rather formal dress for ranch work.

raised prices. "Again we find a certain class of people who only work eight hours per day when they could work ten."[20] With his own workday often extending to twelve or more hours, he was doubtless unable to understand anyone who wished to limit it to a mere eight. But those close to him remembered gentler traits: a man who enjoyed good food so much that he sometimes ate dessert first and kept tea cakes in his pocket, a husband and father who was never too tired to spend time with his family, a man who could tell wonderful jokes and family stories, remaining down-to-earth in spite of his wealth and position. After one of Ida's elaborate Sunday dinners, served formally in the dining room, the entire group would adjourn to the library. There, while the women sat sedately and talked, WPH and the other men would stretch out on the floor and go to sleep.[21]

More than anything else, WPH was considered an astute business-man who generously provided for his family and adeptly steered his business interests through good times and bad. Throughout the 1920s, the McFaddins continued to administer their farming, ranching, oil, and real estate interests. Even though agriculture was suffering a slump, other areas of the economy, particularly oil, were healthy. In 1925, oil was found on the flanks of the old Spindletop Field, and the economy received an enormous boost. As before, the McFaddins profited from their ownership of lands around Spindletop.

Because of the economic momentum of the second Spindletop boom, the Depression that paralyzed the nation after the stock market crash of 1929 did not seriously affect Beaumont until about 1931.[22] Finally, however, the local economy ground to a halt, and even the McFaddin family felt the force of it. In spite of his financial problems, W. P. H. McFaddin, now in failing health, clung to his vast Jefferson and Knox County ranches. "You keep your land, and it will keep you" had always been his motto, and, assisted by sons Perry and Caldwell, he was able to follow his own advice.[23]

On November 5, 1935, his daughter Mamie's birthday, W. P. H. McFaddin died, and for the rest of Mamie's life the occasion was touched with sorrow. Afterward, she devoted her full attention to her mother and husband, and to the home she had lived in since 1907.[24]

In 1950, after several months of illness, Ida McFaddin died. A heartbroken Mamie, who had hardly left her bedside, mourned, "No girl ever loved a mother as I did mine."[25] She buried her mother next to her father in the family plot at Magnolia Cemetery.

For the next eleven years Mamie and Carroll continued to live in the McFaddin home. In 1939 Carroll had built an ice skating rink adjacent to the ice company and called it the Texas Ice Palace. For several years it was a popular place, not only to skate but to see ice shows and even watch the professional hockey team Carroll sponsored, the Texas Rangers. The Ice Palace closed around 1947, but Carroll continued to run the Ice Company until 1951, when he sold it to his brother Levy and turned his attention to cattle raising and rice farming. In 1961

Carroll died, leaving Mamie alone in the McFaddin house. They had remained childless throughout their marriage.[26]

In 1969 the McFaddin family sold most of the Jefferson County ranch land; a large tract of this land eventually became Sea Rim State Park. The Knox County ranch was sold in 1979. The family still retained considerable land holdings, but the vast McFaddin land empire, begun more than a hundred years before when James settled in Jefferson County, augmented by his son William, and fought for so fiercely by his grandson WPH, had at last been dismantled.[27]

After Carroll died, Mamie continued to devote a great deal of time to her home, spending four to six weeks cleaning it each fall and spring, striving to preserve its beauty and elegance. She enjoyed entertaining, too, and was proud to invite friends and acquaintances to the home she loved. Gradually, however, she began to direct even more of her energies outward, and in her later years turned increasingly to philanthropy. She made generous donations to St. Mark's Episcopal Church, All Saints' Episcopal School, Lamar University, St. Elizabeth Hospital, and the Texas Heart Institute in Houston. Her benevolence in her final years brought the McFaddin and Ward names to the attention of a new generation of southeast Texans. She died on October 24, 1982, just short of her eighty-seventh birthday, leaving in her will provisions for turning her home into a museum.

4.
INTERIORS AND COLLECTIONS

MAMIE AND HER FAMILY left for the museum a lifetime's accumulation of items, some purchased, some not. She and her mother enjoyed shopping and bought what they liked and wanted, not limiting themselves to need. Many of their possessions were, of course, gifts or inheritances. And fortunately, they disposed of little. The result is a diverse collection of goods that offers more than just a clue to the McFaddins' and Wards' lives and life-styles at 1906 McFaddin Avenue. It is a well-rounded historical collection containing many examples of contemporary decorative arts, hundreds of mundane and personal items, and plenty of photographs, invoices, diaries, and letters, which richly describe the private lives of the inhabitants of the house.

Various forms, materials, and eras are represented among the approximately 30,000 objects (excluding the thousands of paper documents) in the collection, which spans a date range of more than 150 years.[1] While the collection contains decorative arts representing nineteenth- and twentieth-century styles of silver, furniture, glassware, ceramics, and textiles, it also includes many personal and functional items, such as handkerchiefs and hair pieces, mouse traps and medals, pots and pans. Hundreds of books in the collection reveal not only the family's literary interests but also the importance of books as symbols of a cultured home. Large portraits of family members hang throughout the house and, along with the more than one hundred Oriental rugs, contribute to the decorative nature of the home today as they did during its use as a family dwelling.

In addition to three-dimensional artifacts, there is an extensive collection of family papers. These letters, diaries, invoices, scrapbooks, photographs, and ledgers document not only the family's life-style and activities, but the origins of a large percentage of its possessions. In many cases, Mamie wrote notes on the documents or attached notes to the objects to provide additional information, such as for or by whom the pieces were acquired, where they were meant to be displayed, or what eventually became of them. Such documentation reveals details that bring special significance to objects or provide a view of the McFaddins within a wider national and world context. For instance, a set of silk long underwear in the collection was WPH's wedding underwear, and Ida received two silver Francis I bowls as Christmas gifts one year from her daughter. Mamie bought her first pair of nylon stockings in May 1940; Carroll Ward liked to hit golf balls in the yard; and Mamie and Ida had to return early from their trip to Europe in 1938 because of the threat of World War II.[2] The McFaddin-Ward House collection, then, is more than a group of objects; it is itself a primary source that tells of the life of one family and, in turn, reveals aspects of many people's lives and homes over the course of almost one hundred years.

The McFaddins were not antique collectors. Ida and Mamie enjoyed visiting antique shops in New Orleans and Houston beginning in the 1920s, but they did not make a studied attempt to amass a grand "collection," as did fellow Texans Ima Hogg and Faith Bybee. The McFaddin women shopped for "old" items that reflected their financial status and satisfied their nostalgia for the past. Occasionally they came home with truly fine pieces, and they even enjoyed collecting within certain narrow categories, such as souvenir spoons and pressed glass. They primarily wanted, however, to furnish their home with styles and designs they liked, old or new.

Indeed, a great deal of their furniture was mass-produced around the turn of the century in thriving midwestern factories. The McFaddins purchased it and other goods directly from manufacturers, through catalogues, and from local retailers. They even ordered their early automobiles from out of state. These early vehicles are no longer part of the collection, but a lavender Cadillac (1969) and a gray Rambler (1961) do remain as examples of local purchases. Local stores always benefited heavily from the McFaddins' buying habits, and the family's

Parlor, ca. 1909.

frequent travels provided additional buying sources. In fact, one of Ida's favorite sources for her clothing was, for many years, Cincinnati. And she and her family came home from many a trip up and down the East and West coasts and to foreign countries with items ranging from tables and chairs to Dresden china and sterling silver.

There are playthings, too. A tennis racket, golf clubs, phonographs and records, ice skates, roller skates, and supplies for painting china are just a few of the items the family kept on hand for occupying leisure time. The largest room on the third floor was furnished as a billiard room with a billiard table so large that now it cannot be moved out through any interior openings. (Oral tradition holds that the Averills had moved it up to the third floor via a shaft that Ida had closed shortly after she moved in.) When old enough, Perry and Caldwell occupied this area until they married and moved away. Few children's toys remain, but a train set and teeter-totter and, in the carriage house gymnasium, a basketball hoop, trapezes, and a striking-bag platform are all reminders of days when young people romped around the site.

More than a few objects came into the collection as gifts and be-

Parlor, 1990. Photograph by Alan Leppert.

quests. Birthdays, holidays, and other special occasions provided ample opportunities for gift giving, and the McFaddins and their friends and relatives did so abundantly. Among the gifts listed in Mamie's wedding-gift book are sets of silver, glassware, and linens, many of which are still in the collection. According to Mamie's records, items no longer there are in the possession of relatives or descendants of the original givers. Not quite so well documented are the objects that came from the estate of Ouida Caldwell Watts, Ida's younger sister, who lived in Huntington, West Virginia, and often visited her relatives in Beaumont. When Mrs. Watts died in 1956, Mamie inherited a portion of the Watts estate, integrating many of the furnishings with those already decorating the interiors at her 1906 McFaddin Avenue home.

In spite of their extravagant life-style, a degree of thriftiness, or conservatism, characterized the McFaddins' acquisition habits. Furnishings that graced the Calder Avenue home traveled with family members to McFaddin Avenue, some staying in place until 1982. They made repairs, of course, reupholstered chairs, and rearranged things. In some instances, they replaced items with newer, more stylish ones, but for the most part the public rooms in the house remarkably retained, throughout the twentieth century, the decorative schemes that characterized them when first furnished. Other rooms, such as those on the second floor, changed more dramatically. Hence, the McFaddins' innate conservatism did not prevent them from succumbing to the consumer spirit of their time and spending their money whenever they pleased.

When the McFaddins began furnishing the house in 1907, the decorating styles they used were in the latest fashion. Photographs of these interiors reveal that Beaumont was not merely a backwater town. On the contrary, the McFaddins and other local families, thriving in the town's new prosperity, followed mainstream tastes and responded to national trends. Colonial revival and Arts and Crafts (also called Craftsman or Mission) furnishings largely typified the McFaddins' approach to decorating. They apparently had no interest in creating a comprehensively colonial or Arts and Crafts home. Instead, they approached interior decoration on a room-by-room basis, choosing a style based on their opinion of its appropriateness for a room's function and, importantly, on the pieces of furniture they already possessed. With these styles, the McFaddins did not clutter their interiors with the bric-a-brac and miscellaneous textiles that characterized Victorian interiors. They arranged them, instead, more formally and symmetrically, as would have been expected of a colonial revival home.

This new approach to interior decoration and furnishings design reflected the era's, as well as the McFaddins', interest in the past. Changes wrought by the Industrial Revolution inspired a yearning for yesteryear, and world's fairs and expositions and other forces helped promote aesthetic trends that evoked a sense of the pre-industrial age. Noted historian and author William Seale has pointed out that manufacturers also saw the emulation of designs by individual craftsmen of America's early years as a way to establish themselves and to bring a sense of legitimacy to their work.[3] Hence, they found a wide and receptive audience by producing furniture based on a wide array of historical (not just American colonial) styles. Renaissance-inspired winged beasts and architectonic forms, complex turnings and emphasis on verticality reminiscent of William and Mary furniture, exuberant motion and gilding from French rococo pieces, and neoclassical delicacy and restraint were among motifs and styles revived and popularized. Whether such traits were reproduced creatively or literally, the McFaddins liked the historically based styles. Several of the rooms, and their components, on the first floor of their home provide apt examples.

The spacious entrance hall, for example, is consistent with the grand, classical scale of the building's facade. Its symmetry is interrupted only by the large brick fireplace on its east wall. A stylistic holdover from the late nineteenth century, the fireplace evokes a sense of the gothic, or medieval, though its Greek key and egg-and-dart embellishments correspond with the more classical nature of other architectural features and furnishings in the room. Seating furniture with rich carving and leather (or no) upholstery is reminiscent of styles from previous centuries. Typical of colonial revival tastes, Oriental rugs have always served as floor coverings here and throughout the house. Initially, the family bought machine-made rugs but switched to hand-made examples beginning in the 1920s.[4] The original copper light fixtures also contributed to the entrance hall's atmosphere of bygone days. These fixtures remained in place probably until the 1920s, when changing aesthetic tastes brought about their replacement with a crystal chandelier and crystal torcheres.

The parlor furnishings also conjure up a sense of history, but in this, the most artistic setting in the house, the influence is the French rococo style. An itinerant artist (whose identity is unknown) painted the canvas-covered ceiling and walls, embellished with gold and white rococo moldings, with a trailing rose motif. (As children, Mamie and her brother Caldwell remembered watching the artist at work.)[5] The gilt furniture in the room appears to be French in style but is American in manufacture. The room's three-piece suite of Louis XV-style seating furniture is attributed to the Robert Mitchell Furniture Company of Cincinnati, Ohio. Detailed documentation exists for a marble-top table (present in the room from 1907), which Ida spotted in that same manufacturer's Cincinnati showroom in 1906 and purchased after the alert sales staff wrote to remind her of her interest.[6]

The family bought a considerable amount of Mitchell furniture in the years just before and after they moved into their McFaddin Avenue house. Not only had the company developed a respected reputation and growing market, it was convenient. Cincinnati was right on

Dining room, 1909.

the train route Mrs. McFaddin took to Huntington, West Virginia, on her frequent visits home, so she was familiar with the Mitchell products and able to make purchases directly from the company. Mitchell had also made inroads into the Texas market. For instance, the W. H. Stark House (built in 1894) in Orange was partially furnished with Mitchell furniture, as was the Moody Mansion (built in 1893–1895) in Galveston. Mitchell also supplied furniture to Austin's Driskill Hotel when it was built in 1886 and submitted an unsuccessful bid in 1888 for providing wood furnishings for the Texas State Capitol.[7]

Most of the furniture in the dining room came from the same source. Except for the first set of chairs, which were later replaced with an Elizabethan-style set, the furniture, large and heavy, offered a stark contrast to that in the adjacent parlor. It also contrasted with other early furnishings and features in the same room. A brilliantly colored, signed Tiffany chandelier once hung over the table. A fireplace and original wallcovering characteristic of the Arts and Crafts movement and colonial-style chairs were also prominent decorative features. This room began, then, without reverence to one particular stylistic theme, and though changes were subsequently made (the addition of a crystal

Dining room, 1990. Photograph by Alan Leppert.

chandelier and grasscloth wallcovering, for example), an eclectic combination of styles remains.

The breakfast room and the music room also combined revival furnishings with modern styles. Intended as an informal dining area, the breakfast room contained pieces of furniture less massive than their counterparts in the dining room. In the 1920s, furniture reminiscent of seventeenth-century styles, from the Berkey & Gay Furniture Company of Grand Rapids, Michigan, replaced that which originally furnished the room. Art nouveau light fixtures (in the form of grape clusters and pond lilies) and stained glass, which had come from Lecoutour Brothers in St. Louis, and a French tapestry frieze add color and a sense of frivolity to the room, which is especially eyecatching because of the adjacent conservatory decorated with stained glass and marble. Art glass, including a lamp by Handel & Company of Meriden, Connecticut, and a jack-in-the-pulpit vase by the Quezal Art Glass and Decorating Company of Brooklyn, New York, add a light modern touch to the music room, which is also furnished with heavy Renaissance-style furniture and a baby grand piano (made in 1905) by Ivers and Pond.

Library, 1909.

Certainly, the draperies in the music room, as well as in the other public rooms on the first floor, are decoratively significant. Like much of the family's furniture, these textiles apparently also had midwestern origins. In January 1907, a local newspaper reported that J. Buckingham from Kinnard & Son Household Furnishing Company in St. Louis sold draperies to Beaumont's B. Deutser Furniture Company and came to "fit up" the McFaddin home. An invoice from B. Deutser dated April 20, 1907, indicates a charge to the McFaddins of $6,200 for "Draperies, Lace curtains etc as per contract."[8] Thus, the McFaddins spent lavishly for window treatments and portieres for their new home, carefully selecting them to blend harmoniously and enhance their surroundings. The draperies, different for each room, reflected the decorative, sometimes functional, natures of the rooms they embellished. The green silk draperies in the music room are, for example, decorated with elaborate chainstitched embroidery and satin lyre appliqués. The colored leather appliqués on the entrance hall draperies depict heraldic shield motifs, a reflection of the colonial revivalists' widespread interest in their heritage.

Library, 1990. This current view reflects the room's appearance after redecoration in the early 1940s. Photograph by Alan Leppert.

The library draperies were the only ones in the public rooms replaced before 1950 with panels of a completely different design. In 1941, Mrs. Ward substituted the original draperies, consisting of green silk repp panels and suede trim, with new ones of pale green damask. It was then that the entire room underwent a general redecoration, supervised by a local interior decorator. Significant changes were the painting of the room in a grey-green hue and the "pickling" of the woodwork.[9] (The "pickling" was achieved by stripping and bleaching the original fumed oak finish and adding a glaze consisting of a light-colored stain and a small amount of greenish-white paint.) Overstuffed seating furniture had already been added. While a few early pieces of furniture remained, the changes effectively transformed the room from an Arts and Crafts setting into one more comfortable in appearance and more suited to 1940s tastes.

In addition to the Arts and Crafts furnishings originally used in the library, examples in the collection indicate that at least one other room was decorated in this style. These pieces, which represent manufactur-

North bedroom, 1990. Photograph by Alan Leppert.

ers such as Stickley Brothers and the Shop of the Crafters, appealed to the McFaddins because, like other furnishings in the house, they were of the latest style. Like the historical revival styles, Arts and Crafts furnishings conveyed a sense of the past, not in design but in their emphasis on handcraftsmanship, another manifestation of the reaction against the mechanization and mass production of the Industrial Revolution. Proponents of the movement advocated integrity of design and construction, hence the simple, geometric forms, absence of frivolous carving and fancy upholstery, and exposed construction techniques. There is no indication, however, that the McFaddins purchased items in this style because of an allegiance to the reform philosophy it represented. Rather, these stylish objects with their handcrafted look served as status symbols and contributed to the atmosphere of culture with which the McFaddins sought to surround themselves.

One of the bedrooms on the second floor is now furnished in the Arts and Crafts style, but the other four retain their 1940s appearances, significantly changed, undoubtedly, from what they looked like in 1907. Ida and Mamie had redecorated these rooms (and the library) in the 1930s and 1940s with the help of interior decorators from Beaumont and Houston. They also purchased many of the furnishings for the rooms at antique shops in New Orleans.[10] Embellished Empire, Empire revival, and rococo revival furniture generally sets the decorative tone for these rooms, along with an eclectic blend of porcelain, silver, and glass accessories. Of course, items predating the redecoration of these rooms are interspersed among the later purchases. A Robert Mitchell bed and dresser supposedly purchased by WPH and Ida on their honeymoon in 1894 are but two examples.

Colors and textiles in the second-floor bedrooms are significant characteristics of the new approach to decorative interiors. The colors in these rooms are not vivid, but somewhat subdued, as in the redecorated library. Mamie referred to certain rooms by their colors (such as the blue room) and the furnishings were meant to coordinate. For each room, for example, there is a corresponding breakfast service identifiable by the colors used in the transfer-printed motifs.

The textiles also enhanced the color schemes and were generally made of rustling satins and taffetas. Regina Incorporated of Louisville,

Pink bedroom, 1990. Purchased in New Orleans, these beds bear a carved, floral decoration designed by Mamie Ward. The ceiling vents were installed with an air conditioning system in 1952.

Kentucky, supplied a number of these textiles, which were character-ized by quilting and trapunto decoration. Instead of going from store to store, measurements in hand, shopping for spreads and fabrics, Ida and Mamie bought from the Hambaughs, traveling salespeople for Regina who measured beds and windows and took orders from the women on site.[11] Other textiles came by way of interior decorators. Invoices from the Harris and West firm of Houston dating from the 1940 redecoration of the pink bedroom (the Wards' room) document the purchase of the floral moire taffeta draperies for that room. Cer-tainly, the colors and textiles contribute to a more delicate and femi-nine appearance, and thus the components of these second-floor rooms provide a dramatic contrast in style to what the family favored only three decades earlier.

Suffice it to say, the McFaddin-Ward House interiors and collec-tions represent change. Neither aesthetic tastes, life-styles, nor inhab-itants were static during the several generations spanned by the collec-tions and household settings. Examined individually and in context, the McFaddins' possessions reveal intriguing patterns and nuances of domestic life in the twentieth century. They also tell much about the McFaddins themselves. And since the McFaddins can no longer per-sonally share information about their lives and their era, it is fortunate that they left their home and belongings to do it for them—in a fascinating, albeit more challenging, way.

5.

RESTORATION

BEFORE SHE DIED, Mamie McFaddin Ward wanted to make certain that her family home and possessions would be preserved and enjoyed by future generations. She had loved her home and spent her adult life caring for it. In her later years, however, she began to be concerned about what would become of it after she was gone. She had seen the fates of the other grand homes in Beaumont. Many of them slowly deteriorated and were eventually torn down; others were converted into apartments and businesses. Mamie could not bear the thought of her home suffering from either alteration or neglect; she would have it demolished first.

At the same time she realized that, aside from its sentimental value to her, the house had historical significance. It was the final survivor of a number of similarly styled mansions that had been built in Beaumont after the 1901 Spindletop oil boom, and her dedicated care of it had assured a high state of preservation. It was, after all, already listed on the National Register of Historic Places (1971) and designated a Registered Texas Historical Landmark (1976). Hence, Mamie McFaddin Ward decided that her home would be well suited to become a museum.

To that end, she created the Mamie McFaddin Ward Heritage Foundation in 1978. At her death, as instructed by her will, she gave the building, the land on which it is situated, and its furnishings to the foundation. She also provided some guidelines for carrying out her wish of making the house, grounds, and carriage house a museum, an educational and cultural resource to be conserved, interpreted, and exhibited to the public. The foundation was charged with establishing and maintaining the museum by providing funding and administration.[1] Although Mamie intended the museum to be its primary commitment, the foundation was also to have the power to support other charitable, cultural, historic, and educational organizations and programs in southeast Texas.

While the will consisted for the most part of broad guidelines, to be interpreted in detail by the museum administration, Mamie nevertheless made her specific wishes known. For example, she had at one point offered her home to a national preservation group but ultimately changed her mind because the group wished to restore the house to the period just after its construction in 1905 and 1906. Mamie and her mother had over the years made many changes in the decor of the house, and Mamie wanted to preserve those changes.

Since Mamie and her family left such a wealth of information about their lives and times, a primary goal of the McFaddin-Ward House museum has been to use these resources for educational purposes. Although various ancillary programs have been developed to achieve this end, the main focus has been the house tour. Trained guides lead guests through the house, interpreting the home and its era, the family and its life-style, and the collection.

To interpret effectively this mass of information, extensive and careful research has been necessary. Soon after a staff was formed to operate the museum, staff members began cataloguing the thousands of objects. People associated with the family—friends, relatives, employees—have been and continue to be interviewed in an effort to increase the amount of personal and practical information available. Courthouse documents, as well as invoices, correspondence, and diaries, provide further documentation of the house as it was in 1907 and as its interiors and contents subsequently evolved. The assimilation of information from these many sources makes possible the telling of a story, and the museum's guides are able to interpret this house and collection in a historical and social, as well as physical, context.

That context spans several decades, and the house represents a continuum of use and change. Since Mamie specified that, instead of being taken back to the 1907 period, the interpretation of the house represent the appearance she and her mother had worked diligently to achieve, the primary interpretive period begins with construction of the house and ends with Mrs. McFaddin's death in 1950. Therefore, while visitors see rooms redecorated in the 1930s and 1940s in pinks and greens on the second floor, they also view very different styles of the 1907 period, with added touches from later decades, in first-floor rooms. They may notice original copper light fixtures that remain in place in the second-floor hallway and compare them to the entrance hall's elaborate crystal fixtures, which replaced copper ones decades ago. This sort of juxtaposition is one of the home's most significant educational features. By comparing styles and forms from different periods, visitors learn about changes in taste, in the availability of goods, and in society.

In striving for historical accuracy, museum officials recognized the need for quality and care in the presentation of the physical appearance of the site. Mamie had been meticulous regarding the upkeep of her home, but she could not prevent all of the damage wrought by time and climate. Minor structural repairs were necessary, as was object conservation, textile replication, and the installation of comprehensive security and climate control systems. In the end, three years of intensive preparation went into the refurbishing of the home.

Repairs to the building itself were minimal. The electrical service was updated to accommodate increased demands made by the new climate control system, though the old service still functions, too. Seamed copper roofing was installed around the porch areas on the second and third stories. All painted areas were repainted and weakened railings repaired and reinforced. The chimneys also needed repairs, either by repointing or rebuilding. All in all, since the building had conscientious residents for the entire period of its existence, it was in very good condition.

To achieve accurate room settings, careful attention was given to interior wall surfaces. Paint analyses revealed proper paint colors for painted walls, ceilings, and moldings.[2] Microscopic analysis in the parlor was unnecessary, however, because the hand-painted floral design apparent in early photographs of the room still decorated the walls and ceiling. Decades of grime and dust obscured it, so the museum called in fine arts conservators to clean it up. After testing a number of cleaning methods, the conservators determined that the safest and least toxic approach would be to erase the entire surface with Pink Pearl erasers. Little inpainting was necessary in the parlor and in the breakfast room and conservatory as well. The breakfast room ceiling was decorated with an oil-on-canvas, stenciled design. An artist had painted rose motifs on the ceiling of the conservatory, but cleaning revealed that he never quite finished; areas remained that had only been outlined but never fully painted in. Conservators were able to clean both of these ceilings with mild commercial cleaners. In all, it took twenty-one people (conservators, technicians, and volunteers) a total of 3,000 man-hours to clean the 168 square yards of painted canvas in these three rooms.[3]

Rooms that had been wallpapered were recovered with papers as similar to the originals as possible. In the entrance hall, for example, a brownish burlap wallcovering was installed to correspond not only with the covering used in the room for many years, but also with the early twentieth-century popularity of such neutral-colored, highly textured wallcoverings. For the front hallway on the second floor, Bradbury and Bradbury, of Benicia, California, produced the multicolored paper resembling the circa 1935 flocked paper. (The replacement paper itself is not flocked because of health hazards involved in the flocking process.) The paper installed in the north bedroom, on the other hand, was a reproduction already in the Scalamandre line, chosen for its general aptness for an Arts and Crafts interior and for the Texas provenance of the paper from which it was copied. Papers for other rooms were chosen with equal care and, where reproducing patterns was not feasible, the final selections were always as close as possible to the originals in concept, design, and color.

The tapestry wallcovering in the breakfast room also required special consideration. In place since 1907, the covering was severely deteriorated, and successful restoration was not guaranteed. The museum learned, however, that the company that produced these wallcoverings was still in business in France. Although the same pattern was not still available in the size needed, the company, J. P. Tapestries, was able to weave the wallcoverings in another pattern deemed suitable because of its association with the McFaddins—among the family's possessions was a circa 1907 tapestry wallhanging in this pattern, "Paysage," which depicts a pastoral scene in colors similar to those of the breakfast room originals.

Such good fortune in having original textiles for documentation was especially useful as the museum entered the process of replicating

Mamie McFaddin Ward, ca. 1930.

draperies for each room. As the draperies became worn or
unfashionable, Mrs. McFaddin and Mamie carefully stored them away
on the third floor of their home. Some of the 1907 originals were still
hanging at the time of Mamie's death in 1982, but most had long since
given way either to her own earlier replications (as in the parlor) or to
dissimilar replacements. Mamie's meticulous approach to housekeep-
ing was undoubtedly a key reason for the longevity of these textiles.
At her direction, household staff had cleaned the draperies regularly.
They took them down each spring, carried them to the third floor,
spread them out on the billiard table, cleaned them with solvents,
fumigated them by burning sulphur or formaldehyde candles, and
folded and packed them away in cedar chests until fall.[4]

The combination of expert local craftsmen and companies commit-
ted to the accurate reproduction of historical fabrics led to the success

of the museum's textile replication program. Companies such as Scalamandre and Brunschwig & Fils provided fabrics and fringes duplicating the originals. In fact, Scalamandre, a New York firm, still possessed the jacquard cards for producing the damask fabric for the 1940s library window and door treatments. Other fabrics were not difficult to match, but locating artisans to produce the elaborate stitching, colored leatherwork, and trapunto and quilting was a different matter. Luckily, museum personnel located such craftsmen in Beaumont's surrounding communities and in Houston.

The approach to the museum grounds was a bit different, though no less lacking in attention to detail or quality of work. Mamie had not been able to give as much attention to her yard in the later years of her life, and plant growth had gotten out of hand. Accordingly, museum officials made a commitment to landscaping but not to restoring the grounds to an exact historical appearance. Instead, their goal was to fulfill the potential afforded by the expansive grounds, which covered a full city block, while still remaining true to historical notions of yard and garden design. Drainage systems were added, rose beds raised, the ground resodded, and flower beds cleared out and planted with blossoming annuals and perennials. Mamie's long association with Beaumont's Magnolia Garden Club was but one indication of her love for flowers and the landscape. The constant care and cultivation that her refurbished yard now receives, as well as the occasional garden tours, are tributes to this area of her interest.

Finally, on March 15, 1986, the McFaddin-Ward House opened to the public. Mamie's dream was fulfilled. Her private home was operating as a museum—not as a shrine to herself or to her family, but as an educational resource where visitors from far and wide could learn, from the example of one wealthy southeast Texas family, about life and material culture in the first half of this century.

NOTES

CHAPTER 1

1. Judith Linsley and Ellen Rienstra, *Beaumont: A Chronicle of Promise* (Northridge, Calif.: Windsor Publications, 1982), 23.

2. Mary McMillan Osburn (ed.), "The Atascosita Census of 1826," *Texana*, I (Fall, 1963), 13.

3. Rosine McFaddin Wilson, "The McFaddin Family: Lands, Cattle and Oil on the Texas Gulf Coast," *Texas Gulf Historical and Biographical Record*, XVI (Nov., 1980), 24–26.

4. Judith Linsley and Ellen Rienstra, "Henry Millard, Forgotten Texian," *Texas Gulf Historical and Biographical Record*, XXI (Nov., 1985), 47–48, 56.

5. Wilson, "The McFaddin Family," 26.

6. Jefferson County Commissioners Court Minutes, County Clerk's Office, Jefferson County Courthouse, Beaumont, Texas, Book A, 17.

7. Benjamin F. Harper to Beaumont School Trustees, Sept. 12, 1835 (copy in possession of Judith Linsley and Ellen Rienstra).

8. Jefferson County Commissioners Court Minutes, County Clerk's Office, Jefferson County Courthouse, Beaumont, Texas, Book C, 222 (quotation), 361. Even though she built her own home, there is no record of Elizabeth McFaddin ever actually obtaining a divorce.

9. United States Sixth Census (1840), Jefferson County, Texas, Population Schedules (microfilm; Tyrrell Historical Library, Beaumont).

10. Wilson, "The McFaddin Family," 28.

11. "An Historic Letter," Beaumont *Enterprise*, Mar. 8, 1901, p. 1.

12. William McFaddin obituary, McFaddin-Ward House Manuscript Collection (cited hereafter as MWH).

13. Wilson, "The McFaddin Family," 29, 31.

14. Linsley and Rienstra, *Beaumont*, 35.

15. Deed Records, Jefferson County Courthouse, Beaumont, Book J, 247.

16. Map Records, Jefferson County Courthouse, Beaumont, Book 1, p. 132, plat of McFaddin (Second) Addition to the City of Beaumont, recorded Mar. 20, 1899.

17. Jefferson County Commissioners Court Minutes, County Clerk's Office, Jefferson County Courthouse, Beaumont, Texas, Book C, 84; Wilson, "The McFaddin Family," 31.

18. Cooper K. Ragan (ed.), *Diary of Captain George W. O'Brien* (privately printed), 36, 37, 41, 58; A. Holst to Oskar Holst, Oct. 24, 1863 (copy in MWH, Research Files).

19. Linsley and Rienstra, *Beaumont*, 54, 57.

20. Mamie McFaddin Ward to June Smith, interview, 1974, MWH, Tape 1; Workbook from Jones Commercial College, St. Louis, Mo., MWH, WPH 10 (W. P. H. McFaddin Papers).

21. Wilson, "The McFaddin Family," 31.

22. Ibid., 31, 33–34.

23. Probate Records, Jefferson County Courthouse, Beaumont, Case 161; W. P. H. McFaddin, *Record of Town and Land Lots*, 1881–ca. 1917, MWH, Ledger 52; Florence and Ruth Chambers to Judith Linsley, interview (typed notes), Sept. 8, 1988, MWH.

24. Wilson, "The McFaddin Family," 31.

25. Linsley and Rienstra, *Beaumont*, 73.

26. "Mrs. Emma McFadden [sic]," Galveston *Daily News*, Apr. 19, 1890, p. 6.

27. Wilson, "The McFaddin Family," 39.

28. J. L. Caldwell to W. P. H. McFaddin, July 7, 1894 (postmark), MWH, WPH 9.

29. "McFaddin-Caldwell: A Brilliant Wedding Last Evening," Huntington *Advertiser*, Dec. 5, 1894, MWH, ICM 16 (Ida Caldwell McFaddin Papers).

30. Probate Records, Jefferson County Courthouse, Beaumont, Cases 245 and 255.

31. Map Records, Jefferson County Courthouse, Beaumont, Book 1, p. 132.

32. Linsley and Rienstra, *Beaumont*, 80, 83.

33. Wilson, "The McFaddin Family," 34.

CHAPTER 2

1. P. J. Connolly, contract, 1896, MWH, WPH 10.

2. "Some of Beaumont's Homes: A Few of the Handsome Residences that Adorn Various Parts of the City," unidentified Beaumont newspaper, 1896, MWH, Drawer 4.

3. "Old Averill Homestead Destroyed By Fire,"Beaumont *Journal*, Feb. 16, 1905, p. 5.

4. Warranty Deeds, Jefferson County Courthouse, Beaumont, Book 92, pp. 218–219, Book 94, pp. 333–335, Book 95, p. 60; "W. P. H. McFaddin Buys Handsome Structure—Cash & Trade," Beaumont *Enterprise*, Nov. 30, 1906, p. 5; "Official List of Realty Deeds," ibid., Dec. 7, 1906, p. 3; "Here and There," ibid., Jan. 13, 1907, p. 11.

5. Bonnie A. Sears (Records Researcher and Head Recorder, Pratt Institute) to Howard Perkins, Feb. 14, 1984 (copy in MWH Curatorial Files).

6. For extensive information on colonial revival architecture, see William B. Rhoads, *The Colonial Revival* (7 vols.; New York and London: Garland Publishing, Inc., 1977). The preface contains a useful discussion of terms used to designate the style. See also William B. Rhoads, "The Colonial Revival and American Nationalism," *Journal of the Society of Architectural Historians* (Dec., 1976), 239–254.

7. For further information about the combination of the Beaux-Arts and colonial revival styles, see Mardges Bacon, "Toward a National Style of Architecture: The Beaux-Arts Interpretation of the Colonial Revival," in Alan Axelrod (ed.), *The Colonial Revival in America* (New York and London: W. W. Norton and Co., 1985), 91–121.

8. "Residence of W. P. H. McFaddin, Beaumont, Texas," *Southern Orchards and Homes,* II (Feb., 1909), 15, MWH, Scrapbook 6, pp. 3V–4R. We do not know the total cost of construction, but early speculations by Beaumont newspapers give some clue. The first published estimate was $15,000–$20,000. "New Home of the Averills," Beaumont *Enterprise,* Aug. 13, 1905, p. 8.

9. "The New Averill Home is a Credit to the City," Beaumont *Enterprise,* Oct. 25, 1905, p. 13.

10. For more information about Barber, see Michael A. Tomlan, "Introduction: Toward the Growth of an Artistic Taste," *George F. Barber's Cottage Souvenir Number Two* (Watkins Glen, N.Y.: American Life, 1982), 4–32.

11. "To Build Cement Sidewalks," Beaumont *Journal,* Oct. 11, 1905, p. 2 (quotation); "City News," Beaumont *Enterprise,* Oct. 19, 1905, p. 3.

12. "In Society's Realm: Are Wedded At Home," Beaumont *Enterprise,* Jan. 6, 1907, p. 6.

13. "Elizabethan Mantels. . . ," *Munsey's Magazine,* XXII (Oct., 1899): advertising section, n.p.

14. "Residence of W. P. H. McFaddin," 14. For a discussion of the term "southern colonial," see Rhoads, *The Colonial Revival,* I, 114.

15. Tim Matthewson, "Remodeling the McFaddin-Ward House" (typescript, 1984; MWH, Research Library), 20–21.

16. Mamie McFaddin Ward to June Smith, interview, 1974, MWH, Tape 1. Mamie indicated that horses were kept in inside stalls and cows in the outside ones. She said her family always had four cows at the carriage house until the city passed an ordinance prohibiting livestock in the city.

17. James Lewis Caldwell McFaddin to Mamie Louise McFaddin, Mar. 6, 1911, MWH, MLMW 43 (Mamie Louise McFaddin Ward Papers).

18. "City Briefs," Beaumont *Enterprise,* July 12, 1907, p. 7. The McFaddins soon bought another automobile, ordering it for $500 from the Royal Motor Car Company of Cleveland, Ohio. H. B. Perkins (Royal Motor Car Company) to W. P. H. McFaddin, Aug. 20, 1907, MWH, WPH 12.

19. Matthewson, "Remodeling," 3–4.

20. Henry Conrad Mauer, architectural plans and specifications, 1912, MWH, WPH 10; Ida Caldwell McFaddin to Mamie Louise McFaddin, Apr. 20, 1912, MWH, MLMW 43.

21. Quoted in Eve Kahn and Walter Jowers, "Sleeping Porches," *Old House Journal,* XIV (June, 1986), 239.

22. Matthewson, "Remodeling," 22.

CHAPTER 3

1. Linsley and Rienstra, *Beaumont,* 83, 86.

2. "Musicale and Dance," Beaumont *Enterprise,* Mar. 17, 1907, p. 4; "Friday Card Club," ibid., Apr. 21, 1907, p. 7 (1st quotation); Photograph of a house party, MWH, Scrapbook 3, p. 30R (2nd quotation); Two undated, untitled, unidentified articles from a Beaumont newspaper, MWH, Scrapbook 15, p. 79V.

3. Rosine McFaddin Wilson, "Recollections and Retrospectives" (typescript, Jan., 1986), 52, MWH; Ida McFaddin Pyle to Jan Reitz, interview, Dec. 19, 1983, MWH, Tape 19.

4. Wilson, "Recollections," 62; Automobile Registration for the City of Beaumont for Mamie Louise McFaddin, June 24, 1912, MWH, Scrapbook 18, p. 6R. The automobile was a new Cadillac.

5. Wilson, "Recollections," 65.

6. Mamie McFaddin Ward, Diaries, 1913, MWH, MLMW 59.

7. Information from Ward descendant Mabelle Martin Bryant.

8. John H. Walker and Gwendolyn Wingate, *Beaumont: A Pictorial History* (Norfolk, Va.: Donning, 1983), 103.

9. Several possible explanations exist for Carroll Ward's nickname, most of them linked to his dogged tenacity in playing football. Perhaps the most plausible was given by Dutch Hahn, one of Carroll's teammates, who was quoted in the *Beaumont Enterprise* of July 14, 1961 ("Sport World by Thad," 22.), the day after Carroll's death: "He was a bird dog out there. . . . It was amazing how Doggie would know exactly where that ball would be next. He won many games for us on dogged pursuit and his rugged ability on defense."

10. "Miss Mamie McFaddin Married to Mr. Carroll Ward Before Throng of Friends . . . ," Beaumont *Enterprise*, May 22, 1919, p. 8 (quotation); Wilson, "Recollections," 73.

11. Mamie McFaddin Ward, Diaries, 1919–1942, MWH, MLMW 59; Mamie McFaddin Ward to June Smith, interview, 1974, MWH, Tape 1; Rosine Blount McFaddin, to Tim Matthewson, interview, Feb. 29, 1984 (quotation), MWH, Tape 26.

12. Wilson, "Recollections," 16–18; Mamie McFaddin Ward Diaries, 1919–1942, MWH, MLMW 59.

13. Unidentified newspaper clipping, MWH Scrapbook 10, p. 33R; "McFaddins to Europe," Beaumont *Journal*, July 12, 1906, p. 2; Ida Caldwell McFaddin to W. P. H. McFaddin, July–August 1917, MWH, WPH 9; Wilson, "Recollections," 20; Travel Journals of Ida Caldwell McFaddin and Mamie McFaddin Ward, 1933 and 1938, MWH, ICM 11 and MLMW 59.

14. Ida Caldwell McFaddin, J. L. Caldwell Co. correspondence, MWH, ICM 3–5; Ida Caldwell McFaddin to W. P. H. McFaddin, July–August 1917, MWH, WPH 9.

15. "Mock Trial: Divorce Case of McFaddin vs. McFaddin Last Night," Beaumont *Journal*, Feb. 9, 1900, p. 4.

16. Ida Caldwell McFaddin, D.A.R. Records, MWH, ICM 11–14; Wilson, "Recollections," 32.

17. Mamie McFaddin Ward's Garden Club Scrapbook, MWH, Scrapbook 14, pp. 2V, 3R.

18. Albertine Parker to Judith Linsley and Rosine Wilson, interview, Feb. 9, 1988, MWH, Tapes 30 and 31.

19. Undated newspaper clipping, MWH, Scrapbook 15, p. 16R; Rosine McFaddin Wilson, "Family Stories as Recalled by Rosine M. Wilson" (typescript, Mar. 1988), MWH, Research Files (quotation).

20. "Why Cost of Living is High," Beaumont *Enterprise*, Mar. 20, 1912, p. 6.

21. Rosine Blount McFaddin to Tim Matthewson, interview, Feb. 29, 1984, MWH, Tape 26; and Ida McFaddin Pyle to Tim Matthewson, interview, Mar. 20, 1985, MWH, Tape 25; Mabelle Martin Bryant to Judith Linsley, interview, Sept. 22, 1988, MWH, Tapes 46 and 47; Mamie White Edson to Judith Linsley, interview, Nov. 2, 1988, MWH, Tape 50; Wilson, "Recollections," 14–15.

22. Linsley and Rienstra, *Beaumont*, 92, 100–101.

23. Wilson, "The McFaddin Family," 33.

24. Mamie McFaddin Ward, Diaries, 1936, MWH, MLMW 59; Wilson, "Recollections," 45.

25. Mamie McFaddin Ward, Diaries, Mar. 22, 1950, MWH, MLMW 60.

26. "Opening of Ice Skating Rink Here Tomorrow Brings New Type of Sport to Beaumont," undated, unidentified Beaumont newspaper article, MWH, Scrapbook 11, p. 23R; "Rangers Play First Ice Game on Sunday," ibid., MWH, Scrapbook 11, p. 24R; James Leon Stevenson to Judith Linsley, interview, Sept. 7, 1989, MWH, Tape 62; "Carroll Ward Sells Interest in Ice Firm to Brother," undated, unidentified newspaper article, MWH, Scrapbook 11, p. 26R; "C. E. Ward of Pioneer Family Dies," Beaumont *Journal*, July 13, 1961.

27. "We'll Have 2nd-Largest Texas Park," Beaumont *Enterprise*, July 8, 1972, p. 1.

CHAPTER 4

1. One of the earliest items in the collection is a silver marrow spoon made in England, ca. 1785.

2. Mamie McFaddin Ward, Diaries, 1938–1946, MWH, MLMW 59–60.

3. Ulysses Dietz, "Free-style Colonial: Changing Perceptions and Predilections in Colonial Revival Furniture, 1876–1926 (typescript of lecture presented at Williamsburg Antiques Forum, Feb., 1987) is a good analysis of the origins and popularity of colonial revival style of furniture. William Seale, *The Tasteful Interlude: American Interiors through the Camera's Eye, 1860–1917* (2nd ed., rev.; Nashville: American Association for State and Local History, 1981), 15.

4. Analysis of the collection's 106 Oriental rugs by Tim Matthewson, supported by information from author and rug historian Murray Eiland. See also Tim Matthewson, "Oriental Rugs" (videotaped lecture, Nov. 27, 1985), MWH, Videotape 11.

5. Rosine Blount McFaddin to Tim Matthewson, interview, Feb. 29, 1984, MWH, Tape 26.

6. E. Schofield (Robert Mitchell Furniture Co.) to Ida Caldwell McFaddin, Oct. 19, 1906, MWH, WPH 11; Blueprint of Robert Mitchell table #1430, ibid. The table cost $135.

7. "The Driskill," Austin *Daily Statesman*, Dec. 17, 1886, p. 17; Bonnie Ann Campbell, "Furnishing the Texas State Capitol," *Southwestern Historical Quarterly*, XCII (Oct., 1988), 334–335. We are indebted to Bonnie Ann Campbell for bringing this information to our attention.

8. "Draperies for Beaumont Residence," Beaumont *Enterprise*, Jan. 25, 1907, p. 2; "Here and There," ibid., Jan. 27, 1907, p. 6; B. Deutser Furniture Co., invoice, Apr. 20, 1907, MWH, WPH 11. The *Enterprise* also reported on Jan. 13, 1907, that the McFaddins were going to Kansas City to buy draperies. Whether or not they purchased any there is unknown (p. 11).

9. Mamie McFaddin Ward, Diaries, 1941, MWH, MLMW, 59.

10. Numerous invoices from these years from New Orleans shops, such as Waldhorn, The Royal Company, and Manheim's, survive. They list furniture and light fixtures, and in many cases Mrs. Ward added notes describing their intended locations. Mamie's diaries also contain such information. The entry in Mamie's diary for June 7, 1946, for example, enumerates the purchase in New Orleans and subsequent location of several items: a chandelier for the master bedroom, twin beds for the guest room, and a silver mirror for the dressing table. MWH, MLMW 60.

11. For example, see Mamie McFaddin Ward, Diaries, Feb. 5, 1940, MWH, MLMW 59.

CHAPTER 5

1. Probate Records, Jefferson County Courthouse, Beaumont, Case 49924.

2. Frank S. Welsh, "Comparative Microscopic Paint & Color Analysis," McFaddin-Ward House, Feb., 1985, MWH, Curatorial Files; see also Clark Pearce, "Plan for Interior Finishes" (typescript, Sept. 9, 1985), ibid.

3. Anton Rajer and Kathryn Hurd, "McFaddin-Ward House Mural Conservation Project" (typescript, Jan.–Feb., 1986), MWH, Curatorial Files.

4. This information is contained in numerous entries in Mamie's diaries from the 1930s and 1940s and was confirmed in interviews with longtime servant Cecelia Smith.